COWBOY TIES

COWBOY TIES

HUNTER & SHELKIE MONTANA

GIBBS·SMITH
PUBLISHER

SALT LAKE CITY

Tie on first page from the collection of Cadillac Jack.

Facing title page: These Windsor-style ties were popular in the 1950s and sold for between 50 cents and 75 cents. The red one is a ready-tied model. The two smaller ties and the paisley are owned by Hi Busse, who wore them during performances with Riders of the Purple Sage and the Frontiersmen. Red and green ties from the collection of Bo Caudill.

First edition

96 95 94   5 4 3 2 1

Text and photographs copyright © 1994 Michael and Shelle Neese

This is a Peregrine Smith Book, published by
Gibbs Smith, Publisher
P.O. Box 667
Layton, UT 84041

Design by J. Scott Knudsen, Park City, Utah
Printed and bound in Hong Kong

Library of Congress Catalog-in-Publication Data
Montana, Hunter.
    Cowboy ties / Michael and Shelle Neese.
        p. cm.
    ISBN 0-87905-623-1
    1. Cowboys—Costume—West (U.S.) 2. Neckties—West (U.S.)
I. Neese, Shelle. II. Title.
F596.M56 1994
391'.41—dc20
                             94-17387
                               CIP

CONTENTS

Left to right: Hand-painted spur; bronc rider and lasso done in reflective paint; steer roper hand painted in acrylic on sateen.
(Collection of Spencer Kimball.)

ACKNOWLEDGEMENTS

The production for this book was smooth and coordinated. There are many hands in this project and we would like to thank them all.

First, our staff at Studio Seven Productions in Albuquerque:
Douglas Eckberg, Erin Magennis, David Christ. Special thanks to Lori Jacobson for her styling of several of the shots, most notably the cover.

Second, some people whose guidance was invaluable:
Anna Chavira and Rick Huff, who found Hi Busse—the only remaining original member of the Riders of the Purple Sage—and his collection of ties and vintage photographs.

Chuck and Barbara Cooper from Rancho, Santa Fe, who helped on many levels.

Wendy Lane, owner of Back at the Ranch, Santa Fe, for introducing us to collectors Jack Pressler and Spencer Kimball.

Third and most important, the wonderful collectors whose efforts keep a part of Americana alive:
Bo Caudill; Susan Ricker; Mark Cavender; Donna and James Stegman; Bill Holland; Tony and Bob Stanton; Linda Kohn and Joseph Sherwood; Howard Stallings; Penny and Don Colclough; Trista Vrooman; Stacia from Rough Riders; and Robert Hartman, publisher of *Cowboys and Indians*.

We would also like to thank our editor, Madge Baird, for her gentle guidance and publisher Gibbs Smith for conceiving this project.

PREFACE

THE WEST . . .

From bandanas to bolas, the western tie has been colorfully inspired by the heroes of the real West, as well as the heroes of the silver screen.

When we think of the origins of the West, we think of the Native Americans who gloriously lived with the land, and the Conquistadors from Spain riding on top of the first horses in the New World. We think of the *vaqueros* tending the first ranches of the West and Southwest, and the cowboys on the trail drives from Texas to Kansas. We envision the Union and Confederate cavalries marching and struggling for dominance. We see the pickup-truck generation of ranch and farm hands with their mass-produced Levi's and Wrangler jeans riding in a rodeo on the weekend. Then there is the Hollywood West that provides us with a wonderful illustration of the rich heritage of the people and the land of the West that we Americans treasure.

In *Cowboy Ties* we present a look at the history of western neckwear—from the original neckpieces worn for protection from the elements, to the colorful hand-painted silk ties worn by modern entertainers. The collections featured have been gathered from coast to coast and typify the humor, color and beauty of the West. From burlap to leather, ribbon to fancy expensive silks, bandanas to bolas, Spanish to American Indian wear, this is a collection of photography and lore that we hope will entertain and delight you.

INTRODUCTION

There are many schools of thought on when the necktie first came into existence and how it originated. It would be safe to say that the modern necktie was born from the seventeenth-century "cravat"—a French inspiration that demonstrated that culture's flair for fashion. The ties of this period were made of elegant, fine fabrics such as silk and linen and were often accented with lace, beading, jewels and precious metallic threads. Louis XIV and aristocrats of his period were credited for popularizing this elaborate form of neckwear.

Fashion and function joined hands, and the aristocratic cravat was soon adapted and modified for the working class, who saw the benefits of soft fabric to warm their necks and protect their faces from the harsh elements. Simple, elongated scarves of wool or cotton were accessible and easily made, and thus became the next step of development. By the middle of the nineteenth century, the cravat and neck scarves were in their heyday—there were a wide array of colors and fabrics from which to choose.

The string, or ribbon, tie came on the scene following the Civil War. The simplicity of the string tie allowed many more people to express their fashion flair. Due to its needing only a small amount of material and the ease of fabrication, this "look" soon became the status quo for any dandy gentleman. The string tie was strictly ornamental and was considered the fashion of the day. Years later, it was even tied into a tidy bow for a more formal, dashing look.

On the other side of life came the colorful bandana—a working man's friend. Originally worn to protect necks from the scorching sun and dripping rain, this colorful square of cloth was found to be handy in dozens of situations. For instance, it was used to mop a man's brow, mask his face on a dusty cattle drive, bandage his wound from a gun fight, and spruce up his denim shirt at a square dance.

Sometime before the turn of the century, the more streamlined hanging tie was created. Although women have borrowed its look from time to time for a more tailored and savvy costume statement, men have universally held onto it as their one lasting fashion accessory.

The necktie has gone through thousands of colorful adaptations over the years. Specifically, we are interested here in celebrating the cowboy-design and western-flavor art pieces that have hung around men's necks.

The 1940s through the 1960s were the most prolific years for western decorations on neckties. Those of us who are old enough to remember will never forget the incredible popularity during these years of such western heroes as Gene Autry, Roy Rogers, and Hopalong Cassidy, who gained fame as singing cowboys and eventually made their way to the silver screen and television. Their colorful shirts, hats, and boots were copied by all their die-hard fans and were issued in modified versions for children. But of all the items of clothing, the humorous western ties were the most popular because they could lighten any mood and fit well with any wardrobe. Square-dance ties, bow ties and children's ties all featured their heroes. The quality of these souvenir ties varied from authentic silk to acetate and novelty fabrics which were introduced in the 1940s.

In the 1950s, catalog shopping became all the rage—at least among people who lived in the rural areas. The Miller Stockman Supply Company in Denver advertised western "ready-tieds" for men and ladies. These were short, narrow pieces with Windsor knots on adjustable neckbands. Prices ranged from fifty cents for a simple solid-color rayon tie to a dollar for a four-color embroidered or hand-painted tie, and on the high end, a dollar twenty-five for a leatherette laced tie.

The width of the tie was always changing. At times ties were as narrow as string ties, and by the late 1960s as wide as five inches across, decorated with sequins, gold rope and appliqués. Many of the ties were hand painted by famous western artists such as Til Goodan, Holly Vogue, Olya Grimes, Adrian of California and many more. A variety of motifs included ropes, horse heads, steer heads, square dancers, campfires, brands, bucking broncos, wagon trains, and stage coaches.

The western craze petered out for about a decade, but popular movies such as *Midnight Cowboy, Butch Cassidy and the Sundance Kid* and the all-time '70s classic *Urban Cowboy* were largely responsible for revitalizing the western image in the public's eye. The line dance was introduced as a contemporary of the square dance, and the bola tie was the fashion look of the period.

Western style has again gained a stronghold in the '90s, and ties painted with western symbols and scenes are available in classy shops nationwide. It looks like this time, maybe the cowboy way is here to stay.

Collecting western ties—like collecting anything else—becomes a passion which is fed by great finds. Although some of their ties could be resold for relatively tidy sums of money, most of the people whose collections are featured in this book are hesitant to part with any of the ties.

Most collectors display their collections on racks or bars. Others store them in boxes to protect their fragility. Some even have special display racks built to show off their prized collections. But almost all collectors wear their ties as "conversation pieces."

Because of the availability of vintage ties in the open marketplace for now, many closet collectors only purchase their needs at thrift stores, estate sales, and flea markets; they won't purchase at retail vintage stores. The value of the ties are set according to rarity, usually under $50 for simple designs. But some of the great ties, such as those painted by Til Goodan, sell for over $100. The hand-painted figural ties of unusual subjects usually have the most value.

According to Don Colclough of Cadillac Jack, "There seem to be a limited number of advanced tie collectors out there. By advanced, I mean dedicated consumers who financially can buy all that they need to enhance their collection. We've only run across three who fit that bill."

Whether you're a closet collector or a western aficionado, the funky ties in this book are bound to delight your senses and bring back memories of your favorite cowboy heroes. So settle in to a comfortable saddle, turn on some cowboy music, and relax for a while. You'll soon find yourself "tied to the West."

Tie on left is by Adrian of California. Next to it is a "Calgary Stampede" souvenir tie painted on satin. It was later copied and machine processed and sold in the 1950 Miller Stockman catalog from Denver. Third from left is a contemporary art hand-screened motif. On the far right, a horse head is adorned with show regalia. (Collection Cadillac Jack.)

The hand painting of ties was begun by individual artists in the 1940s. It was wartime and household funds were low. As a way to earn a little cash, artists painted on fabrics to create the first hand-painted ties. When the idea caught on, many of the major tie companies hired the artists to create lines of elegant specialty ties.

Approximately twenty California companies and individuals did nothing but hand-painted ties at that time. Til Goodan, Holly Vogue, Olya Grimes, Adrian of California are just a few. The major tie manufacturers during that period—Towncraft Deluxe, Coast to Coast National Shirt Shop, Wembley, and Britico—all got on the western bandwagon, creating lines of hand-painted ties with western motifs. These companies were the most prolific distributors of western design during this period.

When the general mood of the country began to change in the late 1940s and early '50s, the hand-painted ties took a back seat to more conservative versions. Now, in the 1990s, hand-painted western ties are making a big comeback, and you can find them in the top western stores around the country.

Bronc riders were a popular theme in the early 1950s. These are all hand painted and hand screened. (Collection of Jack Pressler.)

Hand-painted horses.
(High Noon Collection.)

Four heads appear to be
hand painted on hand-
screened fabric. Tie on the left
is embellished with sequins.
(High Noon Collection.)

Four silk ties hand painted with a theme of horses and ropin'. The wagon-train motif is rather unusual. Makers unknown, but all were done in California. (High Noon Collection.)

Hand painted, possibly one of a kind, features a calf-ropin' cowboy and his horse. The air-brush motif likely indicates a 1960s design. On the underside of this tie the artist painted a voluptuous female nude. Unfortunately, the artist didn't leave a signature. Spurclip tie bars by Holland Jewelry. (Collection Holland Jewelry.)

Til Goodan tie on left. Next to it is a hand-painted campfire with branding irons. Right, a rodeo rider pattern is repeated. (Collection of Spencer Kimball.)

SIOBHAN ELDER, CONTEMPORARY TIE ARTIST

Siobhan Elder's upbringing in picturesque Jackson Hole, Wyoming, was a source of inspiration for her painted images on silk and other fabrics. Siobhan's western design base, tempered with a sense of humor, help her to create classy contemporary western ties and scarves. She and her husband currently live in Montana, where they produce hand-painted ties, scarves, and other clothing.

Contemporary ties, hand painted on silk by Siobhan Elder. Detailed with copper metalic paint. (Collection of Rough Riders.)

Three ties featuring a Mexican sombrero motif. All are hand painted and hand screened. Tie on the far right was signed by de la Vegas and was created for the Hotel Reforma, Mexico. (Collection Cadillac Jack.)

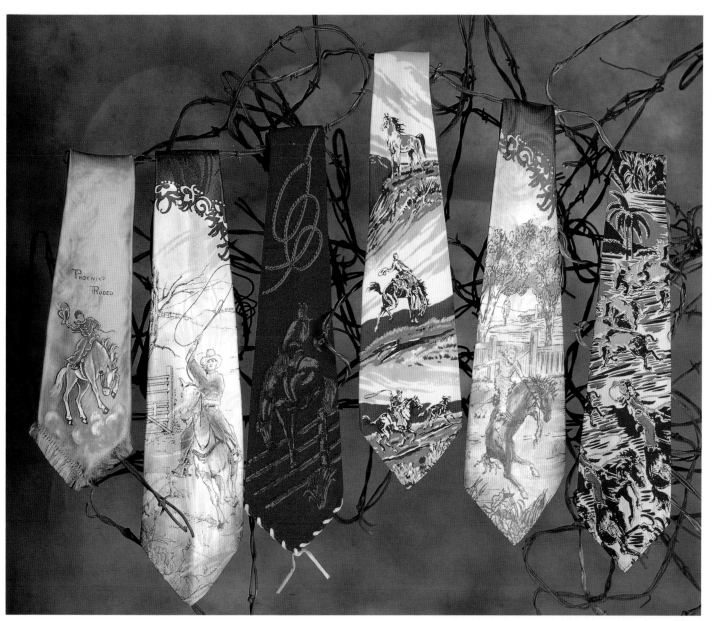

Six hand-painted ties, probably late 1950s designs. The orange sateen "Phoenix Rodeo" tie has an unusual self-fringe. The tie with leather lacing is titled "Saddle Up" and made by Signet. Next on the right is a bucking bronco design by Edwin Megargee. The bucking bronc with trees in the background is handmade by Rhynecliffe. On the far right is a Beau Brummell tie featuring steer roping. (Collection Cadillac Jack.)

"Buffalo and Cactus" by Western Originals. "Pioneer Americana" was made in California by Malibu. "Skull, Cactus and Wagonwheels" by Coast to Coast National Shirt Shop. (Collection Cadillac Jack.)

"The Plainsman" tie on the left has the image repeated on the back. The tie in the center was hand screened by Florida Creations. Third from the left is a California Original individually hand painted by Holly Vogue. Far right is by "California Exotics, Original design hand painted by a leading California artist, Las." (Collection Cadillac Jack.)

All hand painted. (Collection of Howard Stallings.)

Wool gabardine ties. Tie on far left is whipstitched with leather. Second from left is a gabardine hand-painted "catching a horse" and laced with leather at the bottom. The two on the right have hand-stamped horse themes. (Collection of Bo Caudill.)

Hi Busse peeks out from behind Roy Rogers during a 1946 New York tour where he premiered "Don't Fence Me In" and "Along the Navajo Trail." (Courtesy Hi Busse.)

HI BUSSE

As one of the true singing cowboys, Hi ("Hi-Pockets") Busse fell into collecting western ties quite naturally. He was accordionist for Jack Dalton's Riders of The Purple Sage on KFI (1934), the first band so-named. He joined The Texas Ramblers and The Saddletramps before founding his still-active Frontiersmen (1938), who, through band member Eddie Martin, introduced steel guitar into western music. Touring with Roy Rogers, they introduced familiar tunes such as "Along the Navajo Trail" and "Don't Fence Me In." Hi also toured with Tex Ritter, Tex Williams, and Rex Allen, as well as performed on radio and TV. In 1993 Hi Busse was inducted into the Western Music Hall of Fame.

Tie on the left is hand laced, hand painted, and hand studded. In the middle is a fancy hand-painted boot and saddle motif embellished with gold metallic paint. On the right, ornate saddle hand painted by England. (High Noon Collection.)

A variety of western scenes, left to right: "A hangin' for a bank robber who robbed a Wells Fargo stagecoach"; rancher herding cattle; a mining camp scene; a square dance and music theme. All are probably hand screened. (Collection of Bo Caudill.)

A ll hand painted. (Collection of Jack Pressler.)

Hand woven and hand painted with steer heads and horses, all fringed at the bottom. (Collection of Bo Caudill.)

All are hand painted with reflective paint, except the lavender tie, which is done with a flat paint. Note its numerous motifs. (Collection of Jack Pressler.)

Hand screened
and hand
painted on satin,
1940s or 1950s.
All have a horse
and ranching
theme. (Collection
of Jack Pressler.)

The embossed satin became popular in the forties and lasted into the fifties. In western motifs, the backgrounds were often pale or muted, with designs painted in darker colors. Although the satin ties were more elaborately decorated than in earlier years, they were still considered conservative. Surface painting became easier due to the smoothness of the fabric.

Silk-screened horse breaking scene is a classy yet conservative style that would have been worn by Texas bankers in the '40s and '50s. (Collection Jack Pressler.)

Horse motifs hand painted on embossed satin, 1940s. (Collection Off Broadway.)

SUSAN RICKER, COLLECTOR

Susan Ricker, artist and owner of a retail business Off Broadway in Albuquerque, has been a collector of vintage clothing for over twenty-five years. She says her motivation for western tie collecting came about as a result of her passion for vintage clothing and old fabrics with figurative images affixed to them. Susan feels they evoke great design and a sense of history in their personal narratives. She often incorporates the designs of scarves and ties into her paintings.

Inspired by Migritte's art style, this fake wood-grain barn siding is printed on floral embossed satin. By Haband, late 1940s. (Collection Off Broadway.)

Two personal favorites of the collector: "Famous Cattle Brands" in black-and-white on satin. Another symbol of the West—gambling—painted on silk satin and sold at well-known Woodward and Lothrops men's store in Washington, D.C. in the 1950s. (Collection Off Broadway.)

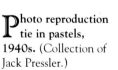

Photo reproduction tie in pastels, 1940s. (Collection of Jack Pressler.)

Unusual combination of minuet dancers and cowboy boots with lasso makes this tie a grand collector's item. Maker unknown. The horse head on the right was painted with leaves, a popular motif of the 1940s. It is hand painted over an underpainting of browns on a blend embossed satin background, by **Smooth Supreme.** (Collection Off Broadway.)

Arden TEXAS PECAN Ice Cream

Novelty ties came about in the 1940s and 1950s. After World War II ended and the soldiers came home, the mood of the country was high. It seemed that even clothing could be a little more frivolous than it had been before. No matter how conservative a man was otherwise, he could go wild with his neckpiece. Tie designers went crazy using gold rope, sequined rhinestones, studs, glow-in-the-dark paint, and even sterling silver to embellish the latest in western neckwear.

Advertising executives recognized the popularity of fun ties and took advantage of the situation by placing ads on neckties. Everything from ice cream to private clubs to rifles and farm implements were pictured on ties along with the names of the companies that sold them. These were often given free to customers to induce sales.

After this period, exotic novelty ties disappeared. Maybe it's time for a comeback. Get out your glue gun and glitter and create your own novelty piece. Maybe it'll be worth a small fortune in the year 2010.

Hand-woven wool tie with embroidered horse head, fringed bottom, 1960s. (Collection Off Broadway.)

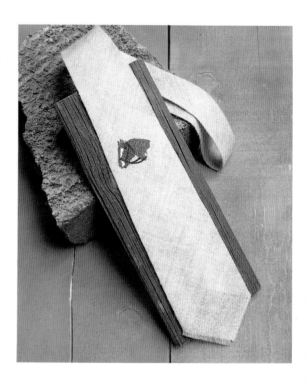

Classic example of an advertising tie, late 1950s. (High Noon Collection.)

The highly embellished novelty tie on the left is of rayon with gold rope, multicolored sequins, and small gold buttons. The horse's head was hand painted. Maker unknown. Right is a hand-painted horse head on embossed silk. (Collection of Bo Caudill.)

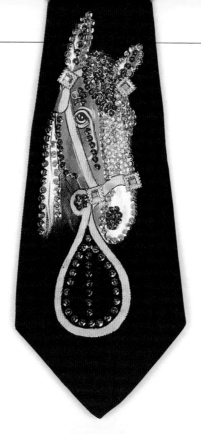

Hand-crafted, hand-painted tie is embellished with multicolored glitter and small gold buttons. Maker unknown. (Collection of Cadillac Jack.)

Left, late 1930s laced leather rodeo tie with Indian stud (collection Off Broadway). Right, hand-tooled leather rodeo tie, 1950s (collection of Jack Pressler).

Hand-painted tie has small gold studs and is hand laced with leather at the bottom. Created by Holly Vogue. (Collection of Rick Huff.)

For those of us who grew up in the fifties, TV and movie heroes ruled our lives. We couldn't wait for the next episode of the Lone Ranger or Hopalong Cassidy. We wanted to shoot like them, dress like them, emulate their style.

To capitalize on this trend, manufacturers created lines of licensed products bearing the images of our heroes. We wore them proudly, and those of us with foresight saved them for our own kids. Today, the children's handkerchiefs and ties are among the most collectible in this category.

Colorful scarf ties inspired by favorite TV heroes—Bat Masterson, Wyatt Earp, Roy Rogers, and the rest—topped off little wranglers' western outfits in the 1950s. (Collections of Jack Pressler and Spencer Kimball.)

Davey Crockett scarf ties, inspired by one of the most popular TV characters of all time. Fess Parker played the role of the "King of the Wild Frontier," and thousands of little boys sported coon-skin caps during the late 1950s. (Collection of Spencer Kimball.)

Motifs based on TV cowboy heroes were stamped on kid-size ties and are now highly collectible. (Collection of Cadillac Jack.)

Children's scarf tie adorned with singing cowboy and bucking bronc rider made any child's wardrobe complete. (Collection of Howard Stallings.)

SPENCER KIMBALL

Artist and collector Spencer Kimball got into collecting for the fun of it. She's like most of us:

"As a young child, I watched too much TV and sat too close to the tube. On weekends, I used my free pass at the Detroit theatre to sit through 'reel' adventures and to eat too many vanilla-flavored Turkish taffy bars. My formative years gave me a love for the 'strange' and a deep sense of humor for the drama in life.

"A few years ago, my boyfriend, Jack Pressler, started collecting and rounding up the trash and treasures from my childhood years, including toy guns and holsters, cowboy radios, old boots and ties, puzzles and cut-out dolls, mantle lamps with horses, and much more. Being a secondhand-store junkie from way back, I joined in wholeheartedly. Just touching these objects from forty years ago brought back a rush of memories and created a flood of images in my painter's mind. Naturally, I started using and abusing all this great stuff in the artwork I made, and it's been a wild ride down memory lane ever since. Decked out in vintage cowboy hat, boots, tie, shirt and skirt, I sell my 'Wahoo Western' paintings at the outdoor art shows in Santa Fe and couldn't be happier!"

*T*n 1949, Victor E. Cedarstaff designed and created the first bola* type of necktie—a triangular slide that he patented as a "yoke." Cedarstaff initially called his design a "piggin necklet," naming it from the piggin-string that the cowboys use for tying the legs of a critter. Later, he was visiting with a friend who had just returned from Argentina. The friend had brought back a device called a *bola* that was used by the *gauchos* (South American cowboys) to catch livestock and wild horses. The bola had three balls attached to the end of three thongs of braided leather or rawhide, which in turn were joined together at their common ends. The similarity of Victor's tie design to the bola prompted him to rename his piggin necklet as the "bola yoke tie," now commonly referred to as the bola tie.

The great attraction of this type of neckpiece is its leather material which lends a rugged, masculine image to the wearer. Traditionally, the western bola utilizes a silver slide that can be accented with stones, inlaid, or stamped with elaborate designs. The bola tie continues to evolve from traditional western use to a mainstream fashion statement for men and women.

---

*This tie is often mistakenly called a "bolo." The *bolo*—a machete type of knife—is the national weapon of the Filipinos and unrelated to the cowboy's costume.

High-end sterling silver and gold bola by Sunset Trails, one of Hollywood's most famous silversmiths. Sunset Trails started as the McCabe Silversmiths of Hollywood, the company that made spurs, ornamental saddle regalia, scarf slides, tie bars, and buckles for such greats as Gene Autry, Roy Rogers, Monte Montana, James Dean, and more. (Collection of Sunset Trails.)

ROBERT AND TONY STANTON

Robert and Tony Stanton are maintaining one of the oldest California silversmith businesses —Sunset Trails. They are preserving the early styles of silver conchas and buckles worn by the Mexican rancheros. Sunset Trails started as the McCabe Silversmith of Hollywood, the company that made spurs, ornamental saddle regalia, scarf slides, tie bars, and buckles for such greats as Gene Autry, Roy Rogers, Monte Montana, James Dean, and more.

Bola ties made in the 1970s by Comstock Silversmith from Nevada, which stemmed from the Irvin Jachens Silver Company that started in 1886. (Collection of Comstock Silversmith.)

A selection of souvenir bolas from the 1950s. (Collection of Jack Pressler.)

Collectible bolas. Chaps on the left were made in the early 1970s. The steer head on the right was made by Visalia Saddlery. Old Visalia pieces can be worth up to $500 on today's collector's market. (High Noon Collection.)

String ties in the style made popular by our favorite western TV gamblers, i.e., Maverick. Left, hand-painted steer heads; right, hand-painted horse heads. (High Noon Collection.)

Fancy clip ons. Left, silver lamé with a boy and girl square dancer (collection of Randall Diehl). Middle, black polyester string tie with metal horseshoe tips (collection Off Broadway). Right, skinny tie embroidered on polyester jacquard with wagon trains (collection of Randall Diehl).

*S*kinny, or string, ties come to mind when we visualize our favorite cowboy heroes from the TV shows of our youth. This style of tie was worn by the Maverick boys, Doc on Gunsmoke, Wyatt Earp, and Bat Masterson, to name just a few. The skinny tie was standard gear for members of the singing cowboy bands such as Riders of the Purple Sage, Sons of the Pioneers, and the Frontiersmen. The skinny tie was also adopted by the square-dance crowd as part of its national costume.

The string tie was easily adaptable to women's wear, and you may recall some of the strong female figures in western movies with an attractive black tie at the neck.

This tie is collected more for nostalgia than for value. Perhaps skinny ties will never make a comeback for everyday wear, but they're sure to show up in new western movies and hang around hoedowns to remind us of yesteryear.

*W*estern style and entertainment even traveled to Hawaii. This 1955 photograph shows a variety of skinny ties, left to right: Tex Ritter in a short scarf; Hi Busse sporting a skinny bow tie; Chief Thundercloud (the original Tonto) in the dark western shirt; Mr. Hall and Wayne West wearing square-dance ties. On the end, sidekick Smiley Burnett is tieless. (Copyright Republic Pictures.)

Ornately designed square-dance ties from the 1960s. Top to bottom: red polyester with rhinestones; ready-tied style with heat-transfer boots and glitter; rust-colored subliminal writing with "Amarillo, Texas"; leather and cowhide fringed tie; brown silk with sequined leaves, stars and shells. (Collection of Jack Pressler.)

Old-fashioned rifles make a nice pattern in this early 1960s tie, screen printed on cotton. (Collection Off Broadway.)

T he 1960s through 1970s was the time when manmade fabrics reigned. Rayon was popular, but it had a big drawback: it shrank when washed. When polyester came along, it became the wonder fabric of the era. Its easy-care, wash-'n'-wear appeal spread like wildfire through all the realms of fashion. A cowboy whose tie was made of polyester could spill beans on it at lunch, lose it in a stampede, retrieve it and swish it in the creek, stuff it in his saddlebag and wear it to the dance later that night.

Design features evident during this time were air-brushed backgrounds and brightly colored fabrics with even brighter designs.

The saddle on the left and rearing horseman on the right are screen painted on rayon. The tie in the middle is hand painted with acrylic. (Collection of Jack Pressler.)

A pictorial tie bar and matching tie made for Don Nesbitt, All-round Champion of the World, 1932. The tie bar was made of three-color gold by Edward H. Bohlin, saddle maker to the stars. (Collection High Noon Western Collectibles.)

The short tie on top is a child's 1950s clip-on. The horse head over cactus is part of a large edition, all hand painted the same—except for different colors—done in a technique much like hand-painted T-shirts are done today. The brown tie features three little bucking broncs (one unseen) and a fence. (Collection Off Broadway.)

Technology brought a breakthrough to the tie industry: the photo reproduction tie. Unheard of before this time, the photo tie caused quite a stir for the industry. This famous Stetson cravat with slip-stitch construction is called "Western Glory." (Collection of Cadillac Jack.)

Hand-painted horses and corral, maker unknown. The drinking steer is a Royal Luxury hand-painted cravat by Wormser. (Collection of Cadillac Jack.)

Indian feather headdress on rayon done in a silk-screen process, made by Raxon. (Collection of Cadillac Jack.)

Hand-painted horse head with glitter is
called "The Palace," by Regan.
Right, hand-painted cowboy boots on an
airbrushed background, maker unknown.
(Collection of Wendy Lane, Back At the
Ranch.)

Steers and steer heads hand painted on polyester were very popular with cattle ranchers in the 1950s. The red tie was hand painted by Evelyn Roberts for Regal Cravats and sold at Hickman's, a popular men's store in Fort Collins, Colorado. (High Noon Collection.)

"Harold's Club" is hand painted on rayon, made in California. The hand-laced tie was made in California and hand painted by Holly Vogue. (Collection of Cadillac Jack.)

Cowboy hat blowing in the wind is a silkscreened tie, by Wembley. The rider with pack horse in the desert is silkscreened, by Pilgrim Acetate Cravats. (Collection of Cadillac Jack.)

Roy Rogers and Gene Autry bandanas from the 1950s. (Collection of Jack Pressler.)

R odeos, county fairs, parades, roundups and expositions are just a few of the special events that have been created to celebrate the illustrious relationships of horse and rider. To capitalize on these occasions, enterprising merchants created commemorative clothing and accessories that were proudly worn as part of the participants' festive regalia. Everyday sun-bleached bandanas and dusty Stetsons were replaced with colorful duds made of specialty fabrics and often custom made for the occasion. The collectible scarves, bolas, and ties not only added flair to the outfits but also served as status symbols and souvenirs for winning competitors and packable memories for others— reminders of the exciting competitions and gala socializing that often marked the highlight of the year for cowboys, who spent most of their time isolated from civilization.

Keep your eyes open for any western-motif handkerchiefs. They are highly collectible because few were made over a short period of time.

TOP TEN REASONS A COWBOY WEARS A COLORFUL BANDANA

✔ Makes a cheerful napkin or tablecloth on the trail

✔ Wipes the sweat off his weary brow

✔ Holds oats for his horse

✔ Protects the back of his neck from bug bites

✔ Wipes his sniffily nose

✔ Covers his face when he's catchin' a snooze

✔ Flags down a stagecoach or a saddle pal

✔ Works as a hot pad for lifting the coffee pot off the fire

✔ Serves as a tourniquet for his wounds

✔ Tied just so, it makes him look extra handsome when he's all duded up for town.

This early 1940s photo of film star Monte Hale and members of the Sagebrush Serenaders shows the ever-popular scarf and bandana as the neckwear of choice. (Courtesy Hi Busse.)

Bandana depicting rodeo life.
(Collection of Jack Pressler.)

(All four bandanas collection of Jack Pressler.)

JACK PRESSLER,
COLLECTOR

An artist, collector, and colorful Santa Fe character, Jack Pressler shares some thoughts on the art of collecting western kitsch:

"I started collecting western neckties and cowboy scarves about 1989 when I got caught up in the latest western craze. I traveled many miles buying vintage cowboy boots, old beat-up cowboy hats, fancy western shirts, and other examples of cowboy kitsch.

"Most of what I bought I sold at a good profit. Since I had been buying and selling neat stuff since I was a kid, it just came naturally for me; but I never really did it to make a living until I realized that it might be possible this time, so I quit my crappy day job and hit the road. I sold about two tons of cowboy boots and about a ton of everything else, and it's still kicking, except I can't find the neat stuff anymore—everyone wants it and nobody can find it.

"I also bought cowboy ties and scarves—anything that had a colorful cowpoke on a buckin' bronco caught my eye. But I got to liking them too much, and something told me to hang onto them because someone someday would appreciate them as much as I did.

"Being an artist has trained my eye to respond to design, color, and overall visual presentation. That's pretty much how I approach and judge physical objects. Is it exciting visually? Are the graphic elements strong? Did the person who made the item have a feel for artistic communication? Another important criteria for collecting is: does it evoke a sense of whimsy and fun and yet retain some historic validity? Because, after all, what you collect has to be fun, don't you agree?"

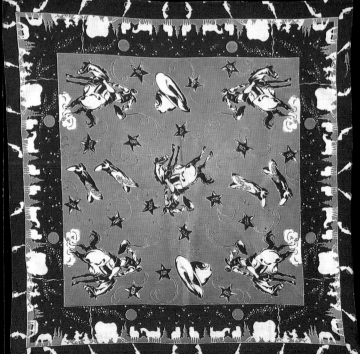

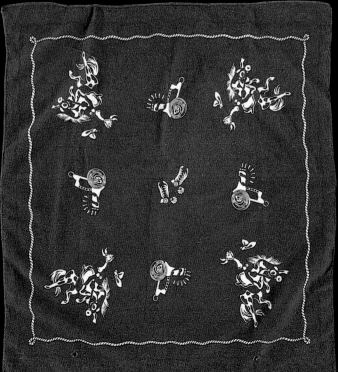

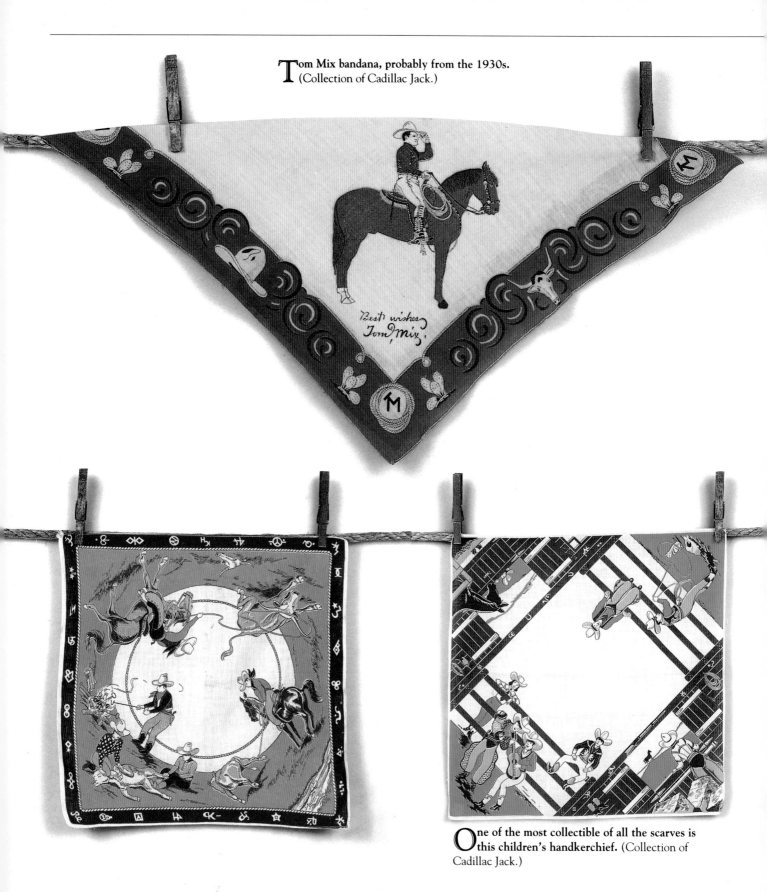

Tom Mix bandana, probably from the 1930s.
(Collection of Cadillac Jack.)

One of the most collectible of all the scarves is
this children's handkerchief. (Collection of
Cadillac Jack.)

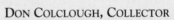

DON COLCLOUGH, COLLECTOR

Don Colclough has made a business—Cadillac Jack—out of collecting. Don was motivated to start collecting neckties in 1972 when he received his first tie, "naked hula dancer," from his grandfather. He began gathering vintage clothing not only for his collection, but for his personal wardrobe as well. Kitsch items such as Hawaiian shirts, cowboy shirts and ties were so well priced in Phoenix, where he lived, that he was able to expand his interest quickly. After twenty years of sleuthing out collectible gems, Don still sees ties that amaze him and is looking for those hidden treasures around the country.

A tie made by the Hamley Saddle Company, associated with the famous Pendleton Roundup Rodeo started in 1910, along with a souvenir scarf from the roundup. (Collection High Noon Western Collectibles.)

Photo realism scarf depicting a campfire, rodeo bronc riding, and branding. (Collection of Jack Pressler.)

ACCESSORIES

*N*o rancher's outfit would be complete without a silver longhorn tie bar, a western bola, a scarf slide of gold, or Miss Rodeo tie pin. Of all the tie accouterments, the accessories are today the most valuable, ranging, for gold and one-of-a-kind pieces, up to $5,000.

So dig through Granddad's old valets and steamer trunks, check the pockets of old jackets, and look in the back corners of drawers to find a few hidden treasures and start your collection.

Hand-beaded ornamental bow tie and bola. (Collection of Trista and Nicholas Vrooman.)

Miss Rodeo Ogden was made starting about 1953 and going until about 1972. She was featured as a pin or tie tack or on a bola tie. (Collection of Comstock Silversmith.)

THE HOLLAND SPURCLIP

The idea of a "spurclip" was born during the depression in 1936. I. J. C. Holland, Sr., a silversmith/jeweler in San Angelo, Texas, wished to give a token of his thanks to suppliers who had extended him credit during those difficult times. This gift of a miniature spur fashioned into a tie clip honored those friends for having "won their spurs" in the true Texas fashion.

The idea was picked up by Houston Harte, publisher of the *Standard Times* newspaper, who immediately purchased three clips from Chase Holland. Harte gave the clips to friends whom he thought had "won their spurs." The first went to Franklin D. Roosevelt, and the other two went to two native Texans then on capitol hill: Vice President John Nance Garner, and Speaker of the House Sam Rayburn.

The tradition of giving spurclips as a special honor has continued throughout the years. All U.S. presidents since F.D.R. have received a spurclip. Menachem Begin, Prime Minister of Israel, was given a spurclip with a Star of David in the center. Actors, sports heroes, and musicians have also been so honored. (Collection of Holland Jewelry.)

A collection of children's bolas that were popular in souvenir shops all over the West in the 1950s. (Collection of Howard Stallings.)

Tie bars from the 1950s. They sold for $1.20–$2.95 back then, depending on whether they were made of sterling silver or silver plate. (Collections of Hi Busse and Mark Cavender.)

HOWARD STALLINGS

I was born and raised in the rural South during the '50s, the golden age of the cinematic cowboy, and like most little boys and girls of that era, I was highly influenced by that imagery.

"As an adult I have always been a collector, compiling impressive collections of phonograph records and books—mostly children's books. I have been concentrating on cowboy memorabilia for about twenty years, searching out the rare cowboy ties from the '30s, '40s, and '50s at every opportunity."

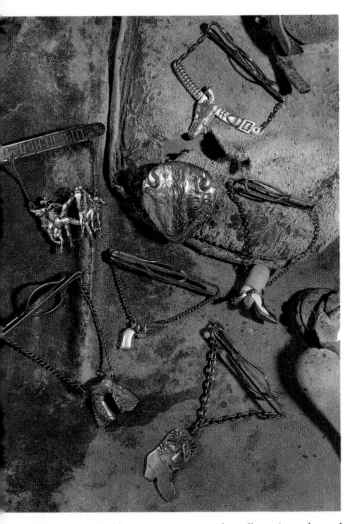

The most valuable tie accessories on the collector's market today are hand-scrolled sterling silver with gold figurines by Bohlin and Sunset Trails. One-of-a-kind pieces are worth anywhere from $150 to $5,000. (High Noon Collection.) The red scarf on the right from 1937 is the most valuable of all collectible scarves because a limited number were originally made for the Rancheros Vistadores, an elite riding group from the Santa Barbara area that was established in the 1920s. The group's illustrious roster included Will James, Leo Carrillo, Walt Disney, Ronald Reagan, Gary Cooper, Ed Borein, and vaquero artist Joe De Young, among others. (High Noon Collection.)

SOURCES

The stores listed below have western ties available for purchase.

ARIZONA

Blondies American Collectibles
Main Street
Florence, AZ 85232
(602) 868-0996
Vintage.

Yippie-Ei-O
7014 E. Camelback Rd. #1020
Scottsdale, AZ 85251
(602) 292-0757
Contemporary

CALIFORNIA

Cadillac Jack
6911 Melrose Ave.
Los Angeles, CA 90038
(213) 931-8864
Vintage.

Gene Autry Western Heritage
4700 Zoo Dr.
Los Angeles, CA 90027
(213) 667-2000
Contemporary and vintage display.

High Noon Western Collectibles
9929 Venice Blvd.
Los Angeles, CA 90034
(310) 202-9010
Vintage.

Jacob Roberts Ltd.
2843 Hill St.
Los Angeles, CA 90007
(800) 421-9083
Contemporary.

Sunset Trails
43205 Business Park Dr.
Temecula, CA 92590
(800) 4-BUCKLE
Contemporary and reproductions.

COLORADO

Crybaby Ranch
1422 Larimer
Denver, CO 80202
(303) 670-0773
Vintage and contemporary.

CONNECTICUT

Best of the West
8 Federal Rd.
Danbury, CT 06810
(203) 792-4743
Vintage and contemporary.

INDIANA

Tonto Rim
2650 E. Tipton
Seymour, IN 47274
(812) 522-7978
Vintage and new.

MASSACHUSETTS

The Western Connection
374 Boston St.
Topsfield, MA 01982
(508) 887-8883
New.

T.P. Saddleblanket
304 Main St.
Great Barrington, MA 01230
(413) 528-6500
Vintage and new.

NEW MEXICO

Back At the Ranch
235 Don Gaspar
Santa Fe, NM 87501
(505) 989-8110
Vintage.

Horse Feathers
P.O. Box 698
Rancho Des Taos, NM 87557
(505) 758-7457
Vintage.

Off Broadway
3110 Central SE
Albuquerque, NM 87105
(505) 268-1489
Vintage.

Rancho
322 McKenzie St.
Santa Fe, NM 87501
(505) 986-1688
Vintage.

Rough Riders
400 Romero St. NW #3
Albuquerque, NM 87104
(505) 242-7564
Contemporary.

TieCoon
Inn at the Loretto
211 Old Sante Fe Trail
Santa Fe, NM 87501
(505) 982-4423
Contemporary

TieCoon
4015 Villa Nova
Dallas, TX 75225
(214) 369-8437
Contemporary

NEW YORK

Whiskey Dust
526 Hudson St.
New York, NY 10014
(212) 691-5576
Vintage.

TENNESSEE

Manuel
1922 Broadway
Nashville, TN 37203
(615) 321-5444
Custom made.

TEXAS

Homestead
223 E. Main
Fredericksberg, TX 78624
(512) 997-5551
Vintage & contemporary

Eclectic
918 W. 12th Street
Austin, TX 78703
(512) 477-1863
Contemporary

Wilson and Mengo Boot
P.O. Box 425
Knickerbocker, TX 76939
(915) 944-4961
Contemporary.

VERMONT

T.P. Saddleblanket
Routes 11 and 30
Manchester Center, VT 05255
(802) 362-9888
Vintage and new.

WASHINGTON

Ruby Montana's
603 2nd St.
Seattle, WA 98104
(206) 621-7669
Vintage and new.

WYOMING

Cattle Kate
P.O. Box 572
Wilson, WY 83014
(307) 733-7414
Vintage reproductions.

The Wrangler
1518 Capital Ave.
Cheyenne, WY 82001
(307) 634-3048
Contemporary.

SPURCLIPS
Holland Jewelry (800) 232-1918
11 W. Beauregard
San Angelo TX 76903
(915) 655-3135
Contemporary

MICHAEL AND SHELLE NEESE (alias Hunter and Shelkie Montana) have lived in Albuquerque, New Mexico, since 1980 and have established their name in the western-wear field of advertising. Their company, Studio Seven Productions, has created beautiful advertising and photography for some of the most interesting clients from coast to coast in America and Canada.

Shelle has a background in the Hollywood movie industry, having worked for George Lucas in Los Angeles when the company was young and small. Michael grew up in the mountains between Santa Fe and Albuquerque. They were married in Los Angeles and decided to return to Albuquerque to produce photography and books.